© Copyright 2023 - All rights reserved.

You may not reproduce, duplicate or send the contents of this book without direct written permission from the author. You cannot hereby despite any circumstance blame the publisher or hold him or her to legal responsibility for any reparation, compensations, or monetary forfeiture owing to the information included herein, either in a direct or an indirect way.

Legal Notice: This book has copyright protection. You can use the book for personal purpose. You should not sell, use, alter, distribute, quote, take excerpts or paraphrase in part or whole the material contained in this book without obtaining the permission of the author first.

Disclaimer Notice: You must take note that the information in this document is for casual reading and entertainment purposes only. We have made every attempt to provide accurate, up to date and reliable information. We do not express or imply guarantees of any kind. The persons who read admit that the writer is not occupied in giving legal, financial, medical or other advice. We put this book content by sourcing various places.

Please consult a licensed professional before you try any techniques shown in this book. By going through this document, the book lover comes to an agreement that under no situation is the author accountable for any forfeiture, direct or indirect, which they may incur because of the use of material contained in this document, including, but not limited to, — errors, omissions, or inaccuracies

BABY SAFETY ADVICE

CUPRINS

12 Must-Have Items to Keep Your Child Safe Around the House 3
A Checklist for Baby-Friendly Travel 7
Auto Safety Advice 9
Crib Safety Measures 12
How To Reduce Poisoning Risk In Your Household! 15
Tips on Toy Safety 22
Your primary responsibility as a parent is baby safety. 26
Auto Seats 27
Tips for Making Baby Food at Home 31
Safe Infant Bedding Procedures 33
Recipes for Baby Foods Safe 34

DISCLAIMER NOTICE

The editor does not guarantee that this content is true due to the internet's propensity to change quickly, although making every attempt to be as precise and complete as possible.

Although every effort has been made to ensure that the information in this publication is accurate, the Publisher disclaims all responsibility for any mistakes, omissions, or other readings of the material. Any perceived disparagement of specific people, groups, or organizations is unintentional.

Practical advice books cannot promise a specific level of revenue, just like anything else in life. It is suggested that readers respond based on their own judgment of their own situation and take the proper action.

It is strongly recommended that all readers seek the advice of certified professionals who are experts in the disciplines of law, business, accounting, and finance.

It is advised to print out this book for reading convenience.

12 MUST-HAVE ITEMS TO KEEP YOUR CHILD SAFE AROUND THE HOUSE

Approximately 2.5 million youngsters are injured or murdered annually, yearly risks in the home. The good news is that many of these tragedies can be avoided by utilizing readily available child safety equipment.

You can childproof your home for a fraction of the price a professional would charge. And safety gear are readily accessible. You can purchase them at hardware stores, infant equipment stores, supermarkets, pharmacies, home and linen stores, and mail-order catalogues.

Here are several child safety gadgets that can avoid a number of injuries in young children. The red numbers match to those seen on the image that follows the text.

Utilize Safety Latches and Locks on cabinets and drawers in kitchens, baths, and other locations to prevent poisonings and other accidents. On cupboards and drawers, safety latches and locks can assist prevent youngsters from obtaining access to medicines, household cleaners, knives, and other sharp objects.

Look for safety latches and locks that are easy for adults to install and operate, yet are strong enough to withstand child pulls and tugs. Safety locks are not a guarantee of safety, but they can make it more difficult for youngsters to gain access to hazardous materials.

A safety latch or lock often costs less than $2.

Use Safety Gates to protect children from falling down steps and to keep them away from hazardous areas. Safety gates can be used to keep children away from stairways and hazardous rooms. Look for safety gates that are tough for children to remove but easy for adults to open and close. Gates that screw to the wall are more secure than "pressure gates" at the top of stairs.

Typically, a safety gate costs between $13 and $40.

Utilize Door Knob Covers and Door Locks to deter children from entering rooms and other potentially hazardous areas. Door knob covers and door locks can assist in keeping youngsters away from hazardous areas, such as swimming pools.

Ensure that the door knob cover is robust enough not to break, yet can be swiftly opened by an adult in the event of an emergency. By restricting access to potentially hazardous areas, door knob coverings could aid in the prevention of a variety of injuries.

The average price of a door knob cover is $1 and the average price of a door lock is $5 and more.

4. Install AntiScald Devices on your faucets and shower heads, and set the setting on your water heater to 120 degrees Fahrenheit to prevent burns from hot water.

By adjusting water temperature, antiscald devices can assist avoid burns.

A typical anti-scald gadget costs between $6 and $30.

Install smoke detectors on every level of your home and in close proximity to bedrooms to detect fires. Smoke detectors are crucial safety devices for preventing fire-related fatalities and injuries.

Check smoke detectors once a month to ensure they are functioning properly. If detectors are powered by batteries, replace them annually or consider using 10-year batteries.

A smoke detector often costs less than $10.

Use Window Guards and Safety Netting to reduce the risk of falls from windows, balconies, decks, and landings. For balconies and decks, window guards and safety nets can avoid serious falls.

The average cost of a window guard or safety net is between $8 and $16.

Use Corner and Edge Bumpers to avoid injury from falls against furniture and fireplace edges.

Corner and edge bumpers can be used with furniture and fireplace hearths to reduce falls-related injuries and to cushion falls against sharp or rough edges.

Typically, corner and edge bumpers cost $1 or more.

Utilize Outlet Plates and Outlet Covers to prevent electrocution. Covers and plates for electrical outlets can protect youngsters from electrical shock and potential electrocution.

Ensure that the outlet protectors cannot be removed easily by children and are large enough to prevent choking.

A standard outlet cover costs less than $2.

Carbon Monoxide (CO) Detectors should be placed outside bedrooms to prevent CO poisoning. A carbon monoxide (CO) detector can prevent carbon monoxide (CO) poisoning.

Homeowners should put CO detectors close to sleeping areas. Included among the households that should utilize CO detectors are those with gas or oil heat or linked garages.

$30 to $70 is the average cost of a carbon monoxide (CO) detector.

Use Safety Tassels and Inner Cord Stops to prevent youngsters from strangling on blind cord loops. Window blind cord safety tassels on miniblinds and tension devices on vertical blinds and drapery cords can avoid strangulation-related deaths and injuries. Inner cord stops can prevent window blind inner cords from strangulation.

Cut the cord loop, remove the buckle, and add safety tassels to each cord on older miniblinds. Ensure that older vertical blinds and drapery cables are secured using tension or tiedown devices. Request safety measures when purchasing new miniblinds, verticals, and drapes to prevent kid strangulation.

Use Door Stops and Door Holders to help reduce finger and hand injuries. On doors and door hinges, installing door stops and door grips can prevent young fingers and hands from becoming pinched or crushed.

The average price of a door stop and door holder is less than $4. Use a Cordless Phone to make it easy to constantly monitor young children, especially while they are in bathtubs, swimming pools, or other potentially hazardous environments.

Cordless phones allow you to continuously monitor your youngster without leaving the area to take a call.

When children are in or near water, such as in a bathtub, a swimming pool, or at the beach, cordless phones are very beneficial.

$30 and above is the typical cost of a cordless phone.

A CHECKLIST FOR BABY-FRIENDLY TRAVEL

When traveling with a baby, you may be so preoccupied with ensuring that you have everything you need to care for the baby that you forget to pack something for yourself. The best course of action is to create a packing list and cross off each item as it is packed.

The following things belong on a sample checklist:

Diapers/ pampers

Blankets

Sleepers

Wet wipes

Baby shampoo and lotion

Extra pacifiers

Bottle

Formula, food, liquid and/or fruit juice

Resealable polyethylene bags

At least one or two additional outfits per day

Nightlight

Seat belt

Portable crib

Collapsible stroller

Sun hat and sunblock Toys

Plastic for diaper changes Any required medications

Additional shirt for oneself

Burping pad

Washable bibs

Feeding spoons

If the hotel accommodation has no kitchen amenities, a kettle is provided.

Packing for a trip with a newborn should commence weeks in advance to guarantee that nothing is forgotten. As you pack each item, ensure that you have added extras in the event of an accident.

Simply walk through a typical day at home and compile a list of all the items the infant requires when not traveling. Add to the list of items. Bring a camera and plenty of film, or if you're using a digital camera, be sure the memory card can hold a large number of images.

AUTO SAFETY ADVICE

The greatest risk to your baby's life, as verified annually by all relevant U.S. government agencies, is while they are in the automobile with you, friends, or relatives.

Here are some guidelines for ensuring your infant's safety while traveling by car.

Seat belts

When purchasing a car seat, be sure to check for;

A label indicating that the product meets or exceeds the Federal Motor Vehicle Safety Standards.

That the car seat is properly installed and will accommodate your child's weight and height

Ensure that the seat you select fits your child precisely Children weighing between 40 and 80 pounds are required to use a booster seat. Rearfacing seats are required for infants one year or younger and up to 20 pounds.

Verify recent car seat recalls before to buying.

Be mindful of the seat belts in your vehicle; not all car seats are compatible with all seat belts.

Consider selecting a fabric-upholstered seat for your youngster, as it may be more comfy.

Susan Dunn's The Best Way to Protect Your Children in the Car

Car seats may be necessary, but there is something else you should be doing to protect your children in the car, as even the bestdesigned car seat in the world cannot guarantee their survival in the event of an accident.

It has been proven that driver mistake contributes to more than 90 percent of crashes.

Your susceptibility to distractions is vital, and once again, one of our greatest technology advancements has proven to be a mixed blessing. You may even utter a highly complex curse.

How about that?

It is the discussion you are having with your sister regarding the upcoming party. Or the quick phone call to confirm directions or to say you will be late. Or, even worse, an intense or complex relationship issue that you and your spouse are debating.

WHILE DRIVING AND USING A CELL PHONE.

It doesn't matter if it's handheld or mounted, or if you're dialing, conversing, communicating furiously, or hanging up. It is hazardous.

In a Fatal Review Reporting System analysis of fatal incidents involving mobile phone use, all cell phoneusing drivers were in what is referred to as "the striking vehicle." This indicates that the driver either impacted a stationary object or veered out of their lane of travel and struck a vehicle or impediment. 75% of the drivers involved in these collisions were engaged in conversation, while 13% were dialing and 13% were hanging up.

Worse yet, one-third of those engaged in conversation were using hands-free mounted phones.

The risk of collision quadruples when using a cell phone, independent of age, driving experience, or prior cell phone use, and – get this – hands-free devices offer no safety advantage.

People who use cell phones just react more slowly and miss information that would help them to avoid collisions. Cell users were unable to prevent collisions with others, even when not at fault.

Your cell phone records can and will be subpoenaed in the event of an accident-related litigation.

When buckling your children into their car seats, why not place your cell phone on the floor near them and turn off the ringer?

Cell phones are beneficial for both productivity and safety. Just make sure you don't use yours to call the emergency services after a car accident caused by you using your phone while driving.

Go to http://www.nysgtsc.state.ny.us/phonndx.html for information on safe cell phone use while driving, if such information exists. And when you fasten your seatbelt, fasten your smartphone as well.

Also, do not absolve the grandparents of responsibility. According to the National Public Services Research Institute for AAA, the distraction effect of cell phone use in the car is two-thirds as great for drivers over the age of 50, and includes all tasks, including placing calls, simple talks, and sophisticated conversations. They lengthen response time by 0.338 percent.

Considering these figures, can legislation be far behind? But do you require legislation to do the right thing?

Susan Dunn, MA, Emotional Intelligence Coach, www.susan.cc Personal and professional development through emotional intelligence coaching, online courses, and ebooks. Susan is the author of "Developing Your Child's Emotional Quotient." For a free ezine, email sdunn@susandunn.cc with "ezine" in the subject line.

CRIB SAFETY MEASURES

Antique cribs with ornate cutouts, corner posts, or lead paint should be discarded.

The distance between the slats should not exceed 23/8 inches to prevent infants from being entangled between them. Cribs made after 1974 are required to meet this and additional stringent safety standards.

The corner posts should be the same height as the end panels or no more than 1/16 of an inch taller.

No openings in the headboard or footboard, so that a child's head cannot become stuck.

In their raised configuration, the top rails of the crib sides should be at least 26 inches above the top of the mattress support in its lowest position.

As soon as the youngster can pull himself to a standing posture, the mattress should be adjusted to its lowest position and left there. Stop using the crib when the top rails are less than three-quarters of the child's height.

Mattress

The mattress should fit snugly next to the crib so that there is no space between them. If an adult can fit two fingers between the mattress and the crib, the mattress must be changed immediately.

Do not use plastic packaging materials as mattress coverings, such as dry cleaning bags.

Plastic film can adhere to a child's face and should never be kept in or around the crib.

Place your infant on his or her back or side on a firm, flat mattress in a crib with no soft covering underneath. Consult your pediatrician regarding the optimal sleeping position for your child.

Crib Fittings

To avoid inadvertent release by the kid, the drop side(s) of the crib should need two independent movements or a minimum force of ten pounds with one motion to release the latch or latches.

Check the hardware of the crib for pieces that are disengaged, damaged, deformed, or loose.

Special inspections must be performed to ensure that the mattress support hangers and brackets cannot fall. The hardware and crib should be devoid of sharp edges, points, and uneven surfaces.

Baby Equipment

Bumper pads must cover the whole interior perimeter of the crib and be secured with ties or snaps.

There should be at least six straps or ties on bumper pads, and any surplus straps or ties should be trimmed. As soon as the youngster is able to pull himself to a standing posture, bumper pads must be removed from the crib.

Damaged teething rails should be repaired, replaced, or removed immediately.

Mobiles and crib gyms that are intended to be hung over or across the crib should be removed when the child is five months old or when he begins to push up onto his hands and knees or can pull himself up to prevent entanglement.

Keep plastic sheets, pillows, and large stuffed animals or toys out of the crib. These can be suffocation dangers or enable children to escape the crib.

Any loose or ripped textile or vinyl pieces must be replaced or mended immediately.

Crib Environment

Place the crib away from windows. Drapery and blind cords constitute a strangulation hazard, and window screens are not designed to keep children out; they are intended to keep insects out.

Install smoke detectors. Follow the manufacturer's placement instructions.

At least once a month, verify that the battery and smoke detector are in functioning order.

Lead poses a health risk, particularly to young children. It can be found in the dust and soil beside busy streets, in old paint on walls, toys, and furniture, and occasionally in fresh imported paint. If you suspect that your kid has ingested lead-based paint or soil, or if you need assistance detecting or removing lead-based paint, call the National Lead Information Center at 8004245330.

HOW TO REDUCE POISONING RISK IN YOUR HOUSEHOLD!

Young children will consume nearly anything.

Keep all potentially toxic liquids and solids out of their reach. Use child-resistant packaging for medicines and household chemicals to prevent poisonings. Each year, approximately one million children under the age of five are exposed to potentially dangerous drugs and home chemicals, according to poison control centers.

Medicines (particularly iron pills and iron-containing dietary supplements), household items, bug sprays, kerosene, lighter fluid, some furniture polishes, turpentine, points, solvents, and goods containing lye and acids are the most common causes of unintentional poisoning in children.

IMMEDIATELY RETURN TO SAFE STORAGE (locked up away from youngsters).

Never leave a bottle of aspirin or other drugs within the reach of youngsters. Return it immediately to a secure location after use.

MEDICINES

When young children discover medicines left by their grandparents, they frequently ingest them. All adults, including grandparents, should use child-resistant closures whenever young children are around. Keep any medications out of the reach and view of youngsters.

Before using any **household product**, read the label and carefully follow the instructions.

Keep these goods out of the reach of children.

Always relock childproof packaging.

KEEP ALL MERCHANDISE IN THEIR ORIGINAL CONTAINERS

Never place kerosene, antifreeze, paints, or solvents in cups, glasses, milk or softdrink bottles, or other containers often used for food or beverages.

Never transfer products into a bottle that lacks a child-resistant cap.

DESTROY OLD MEDICATIONS

Pour the contents of the container down the drain or toilet and rinse it before discarding. Do not discard the container with its contents.

KEEP FOODS AND HOUSEHOLD PRODUCTS SEPARATED

It is important to store cleaning fluids, detergents, lye, soap powders, pesticides, and other common household items separately from food and medications. A fatality may come from a case of mistaken identity.

NEVER CALL MEDICINE "CANDY"

The labeling of flavored drugs as "candy" should not be used to deceive children. When left alone, they may discover the bottle and consume its contents.

GROWING CHILDREN ARE INQUISITIVE ABOUT...

All types of glittering, brightly colored pill bottles and containers. This piques their innate interest. Unless the cabinet is locked or secured with child safety latches, do not store household goods beneath the kitchen sink if a youngster is in the crawling stage.

Before answering the telephone or doorbell, ensure that all bottles and boxes holding medicines or household items are put away if the child is walking.

Find a shelf that is absolutely out of his reach if he is able to climb, or better yet, secure these items in a cabinet or closet.

Always reinsert the child-resistant closure after using a product.

To decrease the likelihood of poisoning:

1. Keep household items and medicines out of the reach and sight of children, preferably in a closed cupboard or closet. Place the container in a secure location, even if you must leave the room for a moment.

2. Keep medicines and dietary supplements (particularly iron pills) in their original containers, never in cups or soda bottles.

Ensure that every product is correctly labeled, and read the label before using.

4. Always turn on the light while administering or ingesting medication to ensure that you have the correct medication and the proper amount or count of dosage.

5. Since children have a tendency to emulate adults, avoiding taking drugs in their company is advised. Do not consume medicine directly from the bottle.

6. Use the right names for all medications.

7. They are not sweet treats.

Periodically purge the contents of the medical cabinet. Flush unused medications down the drain or toilet, rinse the container with wafer, and then dispose of it.

9. Ask acquire and utilize household items packaged in child-resistant containers.

Insist that prescription medications are packaged securely. Retain safety feature securely after use Safety packaging provides additional protection for your children

Poison Lookout Checklist

The locations listed below are the most frequent sites of accidental poisonings within the home. Follow this checklist to understand how to remedy conditions that may result in poisoning. Fix the issue immediately if you respond "No" to any question.

Your objective is to have all of your replies be "Yes."

THE KITCHEN Yes / No

Are child-resistant caps on all hazardous products in the cabinets? Products such as furniture polishes, drain cleaners, and certain oven cleaners should be packaged with child-resistant packaging to prevent young children from opening them by accident.

__/__

Exist original packaging for all potentially hazardous products? If items are not kept in their original containers, there are two potential risks. If a product is accidentally ingested, first-aid instructions are typically printed on the original container's label. And if things are stored in drinking glasses or soda bottles, someone may mistake them for food and consume them.

__/__

Are toxic substances stored separately from edibles? If poisonous substances are stored near food, a person may mistakenly consume the poison by mistakenly ingesting food.

__/__

Have all potentially hazardous products been placed out of children's reach? The most effective method for preventing poisoning is to make poisons impossible to locate and get. Locking all drawers that contain poisonous substances is the most effective poison precaution.

__/__

THE BATHROOM Yes / No

Did you ever consider that, if used improperly, medications could be toxic?

Aspirin overdoses poison a significant number of children each year. If aspirin may be poisonous, imagine how many other substances in your medicine cabinet could also be poisonous.

__/__

Have child-resistant caps been added to your aspirin and other potentially dangerous products? The caps of aspirin and the majority of prescription medications are child-resistant. Check to check whether yours have them and if they are ____ ____ appropriately. Before leaving the pharmacy, double-check the packaging of your prescriptions to ensure that they are child-resistant. It has been established that these caps save children's lives.

Have all expired prescriptions been discarded? As medications age, the compounds they contain may undergo alterations. Therefore, what was once a beneficial drug may now be a poisonous one. Flush all expired medicines into the toilet. After a thorough rinsing, trash the container.

__/__

Are all medications in their original containers with their labels?

Ingredients may or may not be listed on prescription drug labels. However, if the contents are not specified, the pharmacist will be able to quickly identify them using the prescription number on the label. You cannot be sure of what you are taking without the original label and container. In fact, aspirin resembles toxic roach tablets in appearance.

__/__

If your vitamins or vitamin/mineral supplements contain iron, is their container child-resistant? A few iron pills can kill a child, despite the fact that most people consider vitamins and minerals to be non-toxic meals.

__/__

THE GARAGE OR STOCKROOM   Yes   No

Did you realize that many items in your garage or storage space that can be ingested are extremely toxic? It is possible to die from ingesting common compounds such as charcoal lighter, paint thinner and remover, antifreeze, and turpentine.

__/__

Have all of these toxins child-resistant caps? __/__

Are they contained within the containers? __/__

Do the containers bear their original labels? __/__

Have you checked to ensure that no toxins are kept in drinking glasses or soda bottles?

__/__

Are all of these toxic substances hidden and inaccessible?

If you answered "Yes" to each question, you should continue this level of poison protection by ensuring that any potentially hazardous products you purchase have child-resistant caps and are stored out of reach. Place the number for the Poison Control Center next to your phone.

TIPS ON TOY SAFETY

WHEN BUYING TOYS

Careful selection of toys. Consider the age, interests, and ability level of the child.

Ensure that all toys for all ages feature superior design and manufacturing.

Ensure that all directions and instructions are crystal clear, both to you and, where applicable, the youngster. Toys encased in plastic must be thrown immediately lest they constitute a hazard to children.

Be a label reader. Observe age restrictions and adhere to them, such as "Not advised for children under three." Other labels to look for are "Flame retardant/Flame resistant" on fabric products and "Washable/hygienic materials" on plush toys and dolls.

WHEN MAINTAINING TOYS

Check all toys periodically for damage and potential risks. A toy that is broken or potentially hazardous must be discarded or fixed promptly.

Sand sharp edges and splintered surfaces on wooden toys. When repainting toys and toy boxes, avoid using leftover paint unless it was recently purchased, as CPSC-regulated older paints may contain more lead than newer paint. Routinely inspect all outdoor toys for rust or frail, potentially harmful components.

WHEN STORING TOYS

Teach youngsters to place their toys on shelves or in a toy chest after playing in order to prevent trips and falls.

Additionally, toy chests must be inspected for safety.

Utilize a toy chest with a lid that will remain open in any position it is raised to and will not fall on a child unexpectedly. For additional safety, ensure that there are ventilation openings for fresh air. Be cautious of sharp edges that could cause injury and hinges that can pinch or squeeze. Rain or dew can rust or ruin a range of outdoor toys and toy parts, posing a danger to children.

SHARP EDGES

Regulations should prohibit the inclusion of glass and metal edges on new toys for children under eight years old.

However, older toys may break and expose sharp edges as they age.

SMALL PARTS

Older toys can break into pieces small enough to be eaten or trapped in a child's trachea, ears, or nose. The law prohibits the inclusion of tiny parts in new toys for children under three. This includes little, removable eyes and noses on plush toys and dolls as well as small, removable squeakers on squeeze toys. LOUD NOISES Toy caps, certain noise-making weapons, and other toys can make sounds that are loud enough to cause hearing loss. The legislation requires the following label to be placed on boxes of caps that exceed a specific decibel threshold: " "WARNING: Do not discharge within a distance of one foot from the ear. Do not use inside." " There is a ban on caps that can cause hearing damage to children.

<u>CORDS AND STRINGS</u> Toys with lengthy strings or cords may be hazardous for newborns and very young children.

The cords may become entangled around the neck of a newborn, causing suffocation. Never hang toys with long strings, cords, loops, or ribbons in cribs or playpens, where young children could become entangled. When a child is able to pull himself up on their hands and knees, crib gyms should be removed from the crib. Some children have choked when falling across crib gyms that are stretched across the cot.

<u>SHARP POINTS</u>

Broken toys may have sharp points or prongs that pose a hazard. Stuffed toys may contain wires that, if exposed, could cause injury. A CPSC regulation prohibits sharp points on new toys and other items for children under the age of eight.

<u>PROPELLED OBJECTS</u>

Projectiles, such as guided missiles and similar flying toys, can be fashioned into weapons and are especially dangerous to the eyes. Children should never be allowed to play with adult lawn darts or other hobby or athletic equipment with pointed edges. The points of arrows and darts used by youngsters should be made of soft cork, rubber suction cups, or another material designed to prevent injuries. Verify the security of the tips. Avoid dart guns and other devices that are capable of firing pencils or nails.

NOT ALL CHILDREN CAN PLAY WITH ALL TOYS

Keep younger children from accessing toys made for older youngsters. Some toys are advised for older children because they could pose a risk to younger children. Teach older children to assist in keeping their toys out of reach of smaller siblings.

Young children can choke or suffocate if they attempt to consume deflated or broken balloons. More children have suffocated on deflated balloons and balloon fragments than on any other form of toy.

TOYS WITH ELECTRICITY

Toys with electricity that are incorrectly manufactured, wired, or utilized can shock or burn a child. Electric toys must adhere to regulatory specifications for maximum surface temperatures, electrical construction, and conspicuous warning labels.

Children under the age of eight should not play with electric toys containing heating elements. Children should be instructed to handle electric toys appropriately, with caution, and under the supervision of an adult.

TOYS FOR INFANTS

Toys for infants, such as rattles, squeeze toys, and teethers, should be large enough to prevent them from becoming caught in the infant's throat.

YOUR PRIMARY RESPONSIBILITY AS A PARENT IS BABY SAFETY.

After the arrival of your darling bundle of joy, the true labor of parenting begins. As a parent, your most important duty is to ensure the safety of your child. Yet, it is impossible to supervise one's children twenty-four hours a day.

Fortunately, there are a variety of safety items available to prevent children from being injured.

These items include of safety gates, outlet covers, oven and table bumpers, doorknob covers, bed railings, locks and guards, among others. As a parent, you must employ goods that are one step ahead of your children's capabilities. You may accomplish this by stooping down and observing their environment. This provides a kid's-eye view of child safety concerns in your house.

How can you pick which things you need most when there are so many to choose from and so many different brand names? When it comes to safety, purchasing new products rather than old ones is the best course of action. An older, used product may have been recalled owing to severe safety risks, or it may be damaged from previous use. Although hand-me-downs are fantastic for clothing and toys, your child's safety is simply too vital to leave to chance. Babies R Us is a terrific place to purchase all of the necessary safety equipment.

The question of how to pick between, for example, one safety gate and another remains. Here are some shopping advice for some of the most popular safety devices you will need for your infant.

AUTO SEATS

Automobile accidents cause the greatest number of serious injuries and fatalities among youngsters. Hundreds of deaths may be spared annually if youngsters were properly restrained in automobiles. Using a kid safety seat when riding in a vehicle is the best protection you can provide for your child.

When shopping for a car seat, look for the following: A label stating that it fulfills or exceeds the Federal Motor Vehicle Safety Standards; Is the car seat suitable for your child's height and weight?

Be mindful of the type of seat belts your vehicle has; not all car seats are compatible with all seat belts; Check for current car seat recalls before making a purchase; Ensure that the seat you buy fits your child; a smaller infant can slide out of an overly-large seat. Children who weigh between 40 and 80 pounds must use a booster seat; Consider selecting a fabric-upholstered seat; it may be more comfortable for your youngster.

<u>Security Doors</u>

Baby safety gates are an integral part of baby-proofing your home. Now that he's on the go, he has the opportunity to explore every nook and cranny. Your infant is inquisitive about his new surroundings, desiring to investigate every nook and cranny.

Installing safety gates is the most effective technique to prevent him from harming himself. These will prevent him from accessing the staircase, kitchen, or office, where there may be several wires and electrical equipment at his height.

Accordion gates, which open into diamondshaped patterns with broad V's at the top, can trap a baby's head and have caused strangulation deaths. Manufacturers of gates ceased production of these gates in January 1985, however an estimated 15 million gates are still in use. Fingers of young children can become trapped in mesh gates, posing a hazard.

Consider the following when purchasing a security gate:

A hardware-mounted gate that attaches to the doorframe without spaces that could trap fingers or necks. Pressuremounted gates should not be installed between rooms on different floors or at the top of stairs, as youngsters can dislodge them and fall. Swinging gates should never be installed at the top of stairs.

Nonflexible vertical slats or rods should not be more than 2 3/8 inches apart. Sharp edges and protrusions that could injure a child's hands should be inspected. Avoid gates that have structures that could provide a child with a footing for climbing. Keep large toys away from the gate to prevent a youngster from utilizing them to climb over. The gate should be at least 3/4 the height of the child.

Playpens

These enclosed, highsided play rooms are popular because they allow parents to set their infant down knowing he cannot wander off. It's wonderful when you need to answer the phone, do a little ironing, or just take a brief breather!

Consider the following while purchasing a playpen:

Holes in the mesh should be no larger than 1/4 inch to prevent small fingers from becoming entangled; The sides should be at least 20 inches high, measured from the floor of the playpen; Look for padding on the tops of the rails to protect your baby from bumps; The locks that allow you to lower a side should be out of your baby's reach.

Baby monitors

The purpose of a baby monitor is to allow you to wander around your home or yard while still being able to listen to or observe your child.

This can notify you to a crying infant, a baby who needs your assistance, or simply assist you in keeping an eye on your baby while he or she sleeps.

The mobility of the baby/nursery monitor that you purchase will vary. Typically, the base is plugged into the wall in the baby's room or sleeping area. The receiver may be either plug-in or transportable. If you plan to move the monitor from room to room, you should choose a mobile model as opposed to a stationary one.

Consider the following while selecting a baby monitor:

There should be a minimum of two channels to pick from; Ensure that there is a low battery indicator light. Has a poweron light so that you know the unit is on without disturbing the baby; Has a volume control so that you may adjust how loudly you hear your baby; Are you intending to carry your end of the monitoring system? Then a belt clip may be necessary!

Bath Chairs

A bath seat provides extra support for your child in the bathtub and can prevent a soapy infant from slipping out of your hands and striking her head on the tub. Keep in mind, however, that you should NEVER leave your youngster alone in the bathtub!

Consider the following while purchasing a bath seat:

Never use a bath seat on textured or non-skid surfaces unless the manufacturer's instructions specify the seat is suitable for such surfaces; Search for the JPMA Certification Seal.

Always examine the product's features to ensure they match your personal needs, regardless of the safety product you're purchasing. Verify that the product you're contemplating has not been recalled in the recent past. The safety of your child is of the utmost importance; do not leave it to chance!

Claire Bowes is a successful freelance writer and the proprietor of the website babygiftsunique, where you can get additional information on the products sold by babies r us and unique gift ideas. Customized Baby Presents.

TIPS FOR MAKING BABY FOOD AT HOME

By preparing your own baby food, you can ensure that the food your child consumes is fresh, wholesome, and devoid of additives. You can save up to 50 percent of your budget by preparing your own baby food. And to top it off, it's simple; cooking baby food at home is likely a lot less time consuming than you might have imagined.

To create your own baby food, you will require a cooking vessel. A steamer basket is inexpensive, and by cooking fruits and vegetables in it, you can ensure that the nutrients remain in the food, rather than in the boiling water.

You may use a fork, food mill, or blender to puree your food. Almost anything may be reduced to the finest consistency using a blender.

When your infant first begins eating solids, you will puree meals to a very fine consistency, and as he or she grows older, you will create foods with a coarser consistency.

You might want to acquire a food grinder that comes in both large and little sizes. It is both convenient and affordable. The food mill strains most cooked meals to a fairly smooth consistency, while meats provide a challenge due to their rougher texture.

Due to the susceptibility of infants to gastrointestinal distress, you should adhere to the following food-handling guidelines:

Maintain clean hands at all times.

Use clean utensils at all times.

prepare foods immediately after removing them from the refrigerator; freeze meals immediately after cooking for storage.

It is possible to prepare and freeze vast quantities of food. Spoon spoonfuls of your prepared dishes onto a baking sheet. Freeze the drops immediately, then remove them from the sheet and place them in plastic bags once they have frozen. Label and date.

The food can also be frozen in "pop out" ice cube pans made of plastic. Small Tupperware jars with lids perform the same function and can be stacked with ease.

There is a two-month shelf life for frozen baby food.

When preparing baby food from frozen, place the food in a covered cup set in a saucepan of hot water.

Due to their high iron content, cereals are often the first foods introduced to an infant. You can purchase premade baby cereals, or you can make your own by blending oatmeal, for example.

Typically, the next course is fruits. All fruits must be cooked until soft, with the exception of raw, mashed banana. Try creating your own applesauce and pear sauce; don't add any sugar, as these fruits are already sweet enough. Peaches, plums, and apricots may also be boiled or steamed after being peeled.

Utilize fresh vegetables wherever possible to deliver optimal nutrients and flavor to your infant. Canned vegetables are inferior to frozen vegetables.

Steaming veggies is the optimal preparation method. Carrots and sweet potatoes are two well-liked options for the first course.

Babies enjoy eating yogurt, cottage cheese, pumpkin, baked potato, avocado, and tofu (oriental soy bean curd). Blending cottage cheese, bananas, and fresh orange juice is a terrific idea; the resulting mixture is delectable.

Slowly incorporate the meat. They can be boiled or grilled before being placed in a blender with a small amount of milk, banana, or rice cream to achieve the desired consistency. Chicken is typically the first meat that infants are introduced to, and it is generally well-received.

There is no urgency to begin feeding your infant solid foods. His primary food source is milk. You will know when to begin introducing solids to your baby's diet based on your doctor's advice and your own intuition. Always be patient with your infant and wait at least a few days between introducing new meals to prevent allergic reactions.

SAFE INFANT BEDDING PROCEDURES

Place the infant on his or her back on a firm mattress that fits snugly in a crib that meets current safety standards.

Remove any cushions, quilts, comforters, sheepskins, pillow-like plush toys, and other soft items from the infant's cot.

Consider a sleeper or other sleepwear as an alternative to blankets when no additional covering is present.

Place the infant's feet near the foot of the crib while using a blanket. Wrap a small blanket across the mattress of the baby's crib, extending only to the chest.

Ensure that your baby's head remains exposed while sleeping.

Avoid placing the infant to sleep on a waterbed, sofa, soft mattress, cushion, or other soft surface.

RECIPES FOR BABY FOODS SAFE

Excellent Veggies For Children Older Than 10 Months

3 medium potatoes

8 oz. of spinach

2 big cloves garlic

Cube and peel potatoes. Peel and crush garlic.

Cook potatoes, spinach, and garlic in approximately 1/2 cup water over high heat for 15 minutes, or until potatoes are tender.

Combine all ingredients in a blender or food processor and puree until extremely mushy. Freeze in ice cube trays overnight, then transfer to another container and store in the freezer.

Yields 20 servings.

Chicken and Rice Dinner − 10 Months And Over

1/4 pound of ground chicken (boneless breast cut into cubes may be substituted if chicken is to be pureed).

1/2 cup chopped, peeled zucchini

14 cup diced, peeled sweet potato or yam

1/4 cup fresh, frozen, or canned corn

1/2 gram of parsley

1 cup enhanced long grain rice

3 gallons water Instructions: Boil chicken for two minutes in water. Add remaining ingredients. Reduce heat, cover, and cook veggies for 30 minutes, or until tender.

Mix or purée

Chicken Stew — For 10 Months And Older

1 medium-sized peeled and sliced potato

1 glass of Water

1/4 pound of ground chicken (boneless breast cut into cubes may be substituted if the chicken is to be pureed).

1 carrot, cut and peeled

12 cup peeled and chopped yellow squash or summer squash 14 cup cooked barley (see package instructions for processing). Instructions:

Bring water and chicken to a boil. Stir and cook for two minutes Add vegetables. Cover, lower heat, and simmer for 15 minutes with the lid on. Add ready-made barley. Based on the desired consistency, mash or puree.

Tomato Pasta For Infants Older Than 10 Months

1 tbs margarine

1/4 cup shredded cheddar or mild cheese

1 large tomato, peeled and seeded, diced

1 milligram of baby rice

1 gram of cottage cheese

1/2 cup Small Pasta Shapes

Cook the pasta according to the package's instructions.

In a saucepan, melt the margarine and sauté the tomato over low heat for two minutes.

Remove the pan from the heat and stir in the cheeses to create a sauce. Finally, include the baby rice.

The sauce is served over cooked pasta.

Spinach Pasta For Children Over 10 Months

1/2 cup trimmed spinach

1/4 cup shredded mild cheese (Cheddar, Jack, or Gouda)

1/4 cup small-shaped uncooked pasta

2 tablespoons milk/formula

Cook the spinach in a small amount of water for about 5 minutes, or until soft. At the same time, prepare the pasta according to the package's instructions.

Once the spinach has been cooked, squeeze off all extra liquid.

For older babies, combine cheese, pasta, and milk and mix into a puree or chop.

Oatmeal Cookies For Infants Eleven Months Or Older

1 cup enhanced all-purpose flour (for added nutrition, use unbleached or cracked wheat flour).

½ teaspoon baking soda

1/4 teaspoon cinnamon powder* (keep out till your kid is 12 months old).

1/4 teaspoon salt Three-quarters cup vegetable shortening

1 cup sugar (optional, you can substitute ½ cup juice and add an extra ½ cup of oatmeal)

1 big egg

Two or three extremely ripe bananas, mashed (we recommend pureeing them to remove ALL lumps).

2 14 cups newborn oatmeal cereal (you can use plain rolled oats, but you won't receive the additional vitamins. Use 1 34 cups rolled oats and 1 12 cups flour when using rolled oats.

Preheat oven to 400 degrees Celsius.

In a small basin, combine flour, baking soda, cinnamon, and salt.

3. Cream together the shortening and sugar in a large basin (or juice with the oatmeal).

Eggs and bananas are blended into the mixture. Add the dry ingredients gradually and combine thoroughly.

4. Drop teaspoonfuls of dough 1 1/2 inches apart on an ungreased cookie sheet.

5. Bake for 12 minutes, or until browned lightly.

Cool on the rack

Peach Cobbler – 6 Months Or Older

3 peaches in a can (6 halves) OR 3 fresh peaches

1 egg yolk (for infants aged 6 to 10 months, eliminate egg yolk and add infant cereal to thicken).

1 tsp sugar

Peel the peaches and divide them into small pieces.

Blend or mash to the desired consistency.

The egg yolk and sugar should be beaten until smooth.

For infants aged 6 to 10 months, eliminate the egg and add infant cereal by the tablespoon until the appropriate consistency is reached.

4. Bake at 350 degrees for 15 min or until set.

Before serving, chill.

TOFU FINGERNAILS

Slice tofu into tiny cubes

Toss tofu with crushed Cheerios, crushed graham crackers, or crushed oats in a Ziploc bag.

Seal bag and toss to evenly coat the tofu cubes – This can be served as finger food or as a protein supplement during meals.

www.ingramcontent.com/pod-product-compliance
Lightning Source LLC
Chambersburg PA
CBHW070340120526
44590CB00017B/2960